Moons

By Gregory Vogt

OUR UNIVERSE

www.raintreepublishers.co.uk
Visit our website to find out more information about Raintree books.

To order:
  Phone 44 (0)1865 888112
  Send a fax to 44 (0)1865 314091
  Visit the Raintree Bookshop at www.raintreepublishers.co.uk to
browse our catalogue and order online.

First published in Great Britain by
Raintree Publishers, Halley Court,
Jordan Hill, Oxford OX2 8EJ, part of
Harcourt Education.
Raintree is a registered trademark of
Harcourt Education Ltd.

© Harcourt Education Ltd 2003
The moral right of the proprietor has
been asserted.

Design: Jo Hinton-Malivoire and
Tinstar Design (www.tinstar.co.uk),
Jo Sapwell (www.tipani.co.uk)
Illustrations: Art Construction
Picture Research: Maria Joannou and
Su Alexander
Production: Jonathan Smith

Originated by Dot Gradations Ltd
Printed and bound in Hong Kong,
China by South China Printing Co. Ltd.

ISBN 1 844 21415 X (hardback)
06 05 04 03 02
10 9 8 7 6 5 4 3 2 1

**British Library Cataloguing in
Publication Data**
Vogt, Gregory
Moons. - (Our universe)
1.Satellites - Juvenile literature
I.Title
523.9'8

A full catalogue record for this book
is available from the British Library.

Acknowledgements
The publishers would like to thank
the following for permission to
reproduce photographs:
Cover Photo; NASA/JPL, title page;
NASA/USGS, 14; NASA, 16; NASA,
17; NASA, 18; NASA, 20;
NASA/Malin Space Science Systems,
22; Dr. R. Albrecht, ESA/ESO Space
Telescope European Coordinating
Facility/ NASA, 24; NASA/DLR, 26;
NASA/ DLR, 28; NASA/DLR, 30;
NASA/ DLR, 32; NASA, 35; NASA,
36; NASA, 39; NASA, 40; NASA, 42;
NASA; 44

Content Consultant
David Jewitt
Professor of Astronomy
University of Hawaii Institute for
Astronomy

Every effort has been made to
contact copyright holders of any
material reproduced in this book.
Any omissions will be rectified in
subsequent printings if notice is
given to the publishers.

Contents

Any words appearing in the text in bold, **like this**, are explained in the glossary.

Diagram of the Moon

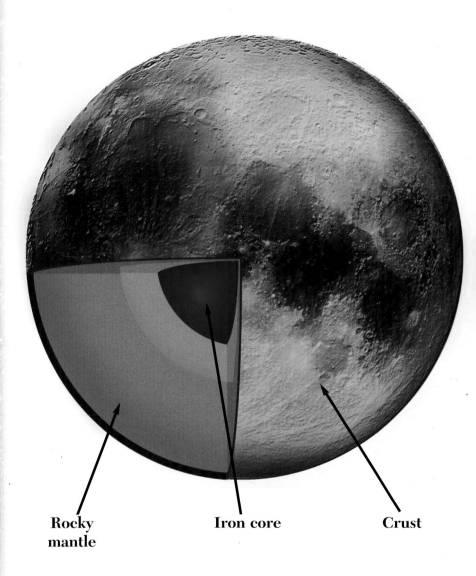

Rocky
mantle

Iron core

Crust

A quick look at moons

What are moons?
Moons are natural objects that circle around planets.

What are moons made of?
Moons are made of rock, or rock and ice.

Do all planets have moons?
Mercury and Venus do not have moons. All other planets have one or more moons circling around them.

How many moons are there?
There are 101 known moons in the solar system.

Which planet has the most moons?
Jupiter has the most moons. It has 39 known moons travelling around it.

What is the largest moon?
Jupiter's moon Ganymede is the largest moon in the solar system.

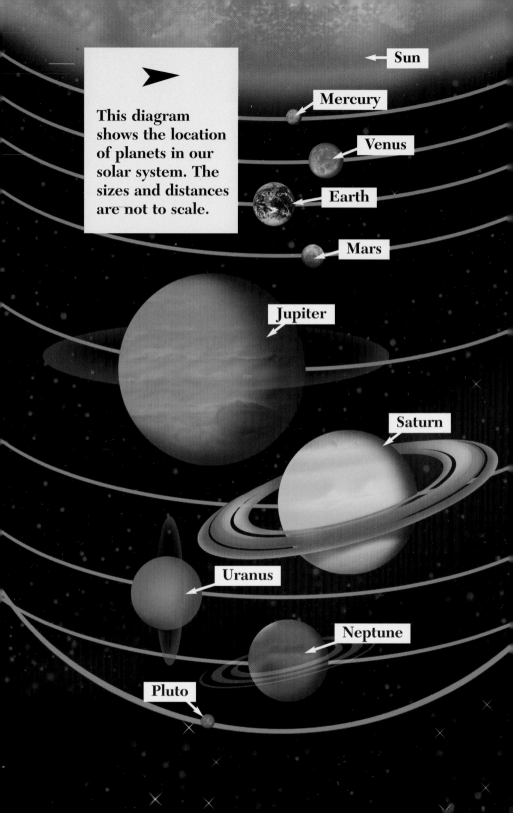

This diagram shows the location of planets in our solar system. The sizes and distances are not to scale.

Sun

Mercury

Venus

Earth

Mars

Jupiter

Saturn

Uranus

Neptune

Pluto

One hundred and one moons

The Earth's Moon is a large ball of rock and dust that circles the Earth. It looks like a large white globe in the night sky. The Moon appears larger and brighter than all of the stars because it is much closer to the Earth than they are.

The Earth and the Moon are part of our **solar system**. The solar system is made up of the Sun and all the objects circling it. Our solar system has nine planets and 101 known moons. A moon is a natural satellite of a planet. A satellite is something that travels around something else.

Only two planets do not have moons, Mercury and Venus. Mercury is the closest planet to the Sun. Venus is the second planet from the Sun.

Astronomers may find more moons as they study the solar system. Astronomers are scientists who study objects in space.

Moons and orbits

A moon is an object that travels around a planet. Moons are usually large balls of rock, or rock and ice. They are smaller than the planets they circle.

Moons travel around planets in paths called **orbits.** Some moons have circle-shaped orbits. Other moons have orbits shaped like ovals. An oval is shaped like a slightly flattened circle.

A moon that orbits close to a planet travels very quickly. The planet's **gravity** pulls on the moon. This force is called a gravitational pull. Gravity is a natural force that attracts objects to each other. A large object that is very heavy and takes up a lot of space has greater gravity than one which is lighter and takes up less space. Such an object is called massive because of its mass, which is the weight and space it takes up.

Planets have greater gravitational pulls because they are more massive than moons. Gravity gets weaker as a moon moves further away from the planet. A distant moon travels more slowly than a close moon.

Moons that are close to planets complete their orbits in just a few hours. Distant moons take much longer. One distant moon of the planet Uranus takes almost 1300 Earth days to circle the planet once.

This diagram shows the different orbits of a planet's moons. The moon closest to the planet travels the fastest. The further away a moon is, the slower it travels through space. The moon furthest away from the planet travels the slowest.

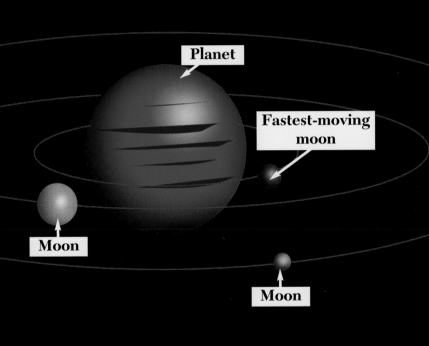

Planet

Fastest-moving moon

Moon

Moon

Slowest-moving moon

The *Galileo Orbiter* took this picture of the Moon. The dark areas are basins filled with lava rock.

The Earth's Moon

The Moon is a rocky ball 3475 kilometres (2160 miles) in **diameter**. It is an average of 384,000 kilometres (238,000 miles) from the Earth. The **gravity** of the Earth keeps the Moon in **orbit**. The Moon orbits the Earth once every 29.5 days, and it takes 29.5 days for the moon to spin around once.

The Moon has a little gravity. The gravity of the Moon and the Sun pulls on the water in the Earth's oceans. This makes the water rise and fall every day. Water gets deeper around the shores of the land. Then it flows back out to sea again. These regular changes in the water level are called the tides.

From the Earth, the Moon looks black and white. It has light grey and black rocks on its surface. The light-coloured areas of the Moon are mostly mountains and large **craters**. A crater is a large, bowl-shaped hole in the ground.

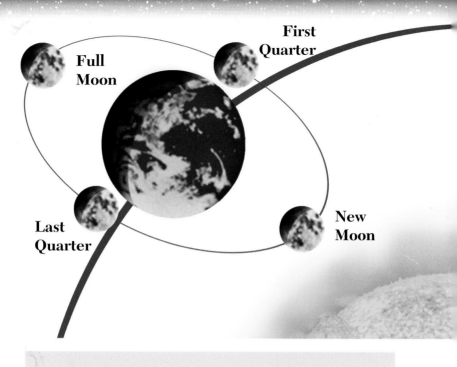

Full
Moon

First
Quarter

Last
Quarter

New
Moon

> This diagram shows how the changing
> positions of the Earth and the Moon cause
> the Moon's phases.

Changing Moon

The Moon is very bright, but it does not give off any
light of its own. Instead, it reflects light. The light
shining from the Moon is really from the Sun. The
sunlight bounces off the Moon and into space
towards the Earth.

The amount of sunlight that the Moon reflects
back to the Earth changes. At times, more sunlight is
reflected towards the Earth. When this happens, we
see more of the Moon. The Moon falls into shadow

at other times. When this happens less of its surface is lit up by the Sun and it reflects less light. This makes the Moon look different every night. The shape of the lit surface of the Moon changes. The different shapes are called the Moon's phases. It takes the Moon one month to complete its cycle of changing phases. Once the Moon's cycle is complete, it starts over again.

The Moon's **orbit** causes the phases. Sometimes the Moon is between the Earth and the Sun. The Sun lights the side of the Moon facing it. At this time, the side of the Moon facing the Earth appears dark. Other times, the Moon is on the other side of the Earth. Then the fully lit side of the Moon faces the Earth.

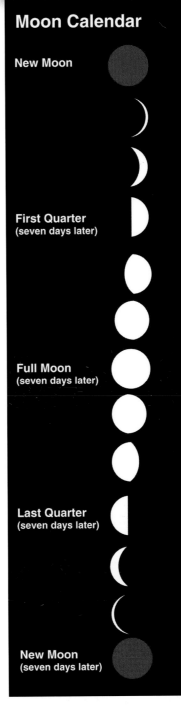

Moon Calendar

New Moon

First Quarter
(seven days later)

Full Moon
(seven days later)

Last Quarter
(seven days later)

New Moon
(seven days later)

13

A meteorite blasted the 93-km (58-mile) wide Copernicus Crater on the Moon's surface.

Meteorites

Small rocks and pieces of dust called meteoroids float in outer space. Meteoroids are called **meteorites** when they crash into other objects. Sometimes meteorites crash into the Moon and cause explosions. The explosions blast some of the Moon's rock into space. This leaves **craters** in the surface of the Moon. Large meteorites blast huge craters, while small meteorites blast small craters.

The blasted rock rises into space and then falls back down to the Moon's surface. It piles up around the rim of the crater. Rays are what **astronomers** call the piles of blasted material around craters.

Very large meteorites make huge explosions on the Moon, and leave large craters on its surface. The explosion makes some of the rock inside the crater melt. The melted rock in the centre of the new crater becomes smooth like the surface of a lake. When the rock cools, it forms a flat bottom.

Sometimes the melted rock in the middle of a big crater splashes upward. The rock cools before it falls back down. This creates a small mountain in the middle of the crater. Only large meteorites cause explosions hot enough to melt rock.

Ancient surface

The surface of the Moon has not changed in billions of years. This is because the Moon has no wind, rain or snow to wear away its surface. Craters on the Moon last billions of years. The Earth has had many craters too, but most have been worn away.

The surface of the Moon

The surface of the Moon is made up of more than craters. It is covered with grey, dust-like soil. Mountains, craters and smooth, flat areas cover the Moon's surface.

Far side of the Moon

From the Earth, you can only see one side of the Moon. It takes the Moon the same amount of time to turn once as it does to orbit the Earth. To see the other side of the Moon, you have to travel in a spaceship. The *Galileo Orbiter* took this picture of the far side of the Moon.

The side of the Moon facing the Earth has large smooth areas called maria. Maria are large basins that are completely filled with lava. Millions of years ago, melted rock called lava flowed from inside the Moon to the surface. The lava filled many large craters and basins. Lava turns into dark rock when it cools and hardens. The lava makes maria dark grey. Light-grey craters surround maria. The Moon's craters are many sizes. The largest impact crater is about 2250 kilometres (1400 miles) across. The Moon's smallest craters are just large enough to hold a grain of sand.

The side of the Moon facing away from the Earth has few maria. It is mostly covered with large craters.

Astronaut Edwin Aldrin became the second person to stand on the Moon during the *Apollo 11* mission.

Moon walkers

Between 1962 and 1972, the National Aeronautic and Space Administration (NASA) ran the *Apollo* space programme. Each *Apollo* spacecraft had two parts. One part of the spacecraft was an **orbiter** that stayed in space. The other part was a lander that was built to land on the Moon.

There were six *Apollo* missions to the Moon. Powerful rockets launched the spacecraft into space. The trip to the Moon took three days.

Each spacecraft carried three astronauts. When they reached the Moon, one astronaut remained in the spacecraft. Two astronauts climbed into the lander. The lander had four legs and a rocket engine. The lander brought them down to the surface.

On the Moon, the astronauts wore spacesuits that gave them air to breathe and water to drink. The astronauts collected rocks and soil to bring home. They took many pictures of the Moon. They also set up experiments to learn about the Moon. One team of astronauts brought a special car to drive on the Moon.

The astronauts returned to the orbiter when they had finished exploring the Moon. Then the spacecraft rocketed back to the Earth.

Flowing lava cut this channel, which is more than 100-km (60-mile) long. It is called the Hadley Rille. An astronaut took this photograph of the Hadley Rille on the Moon.

Where the Moon came from

In total, the *Apollo* astronauts brought home 382 kilogrammes of Moon rocks for scientists to study. They had many questions about the Moon that they wanted to answer.

Scientists wanted to find out the age of the Moon. They studied moon rocks and learned that it is more than 4.5 billion years old.

Scientists wanted to know what the Moon was made of. They discovered that moon rocks are made of many elements, such as the metals iron and titanium. Elements are pure materials found in nature. Moon rocks are a lot like lava rocks on the Earth.

Scientists also wanted to know where the Moon came from. They are still not sure how the Moon formed, but some scientists think the Earth was once struck by a huge **meteorite**. Most of the meteorite became part of the Earth, but the explosion blasted pieces of the meteorite and the Earth into space. Scientists believe that over millions of years, these pieces joined together and formed the Moon.

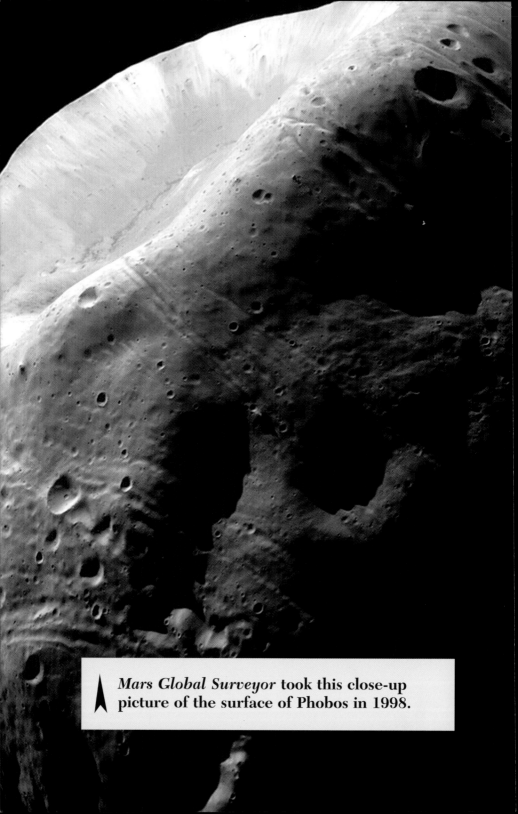

Mars Global Surveyor took this close-up picture of the surface of Phobos in 1998.

Moons of Mars and Pluto

O ur **solar system** has two main kinds of planets. Five planets are made of rock. The rocky planets are Mercury, Venus, Earth, Mars and Pluto. Mars has the most moons of the rocky planets.

Mars has two moons called Phobos and Deimos. Both are shaped like giant potatoes. They each have many small **craters** on their rocky surfaces.

The moons are very small and are hard to see from the Earth. Phobos is only 27 kilometres (17 miles) in **diameter**. Deimos is even smaller. It is only 15 kilometres (9.3 miles) in diameter.

Phobos **orbits** 9378 kilometres (5827 miles) above Mars. It circles the planet once every 7.6 hours. Deimos orbits 23,459 kilometres (14,577 miles) above Mars. It circles the planet once every 30 hours.

The Hubble Space Telescope took the clearest picture of Pluto (left) and Charon (right) in 1994.

Pluto and Charon

Pluto was named after the Greek god of the dead. Pluto is a cold, dark place because it is the furthest planet from the Sun. Little sunlight reaches the surface of Pluto. It is more than 30 times further from the Sun than the Earth.

In 1978, **astronomer** James Christy from the USA found a moon **orbiting** Pluto. He named it Charon. In Greek stories, Charon was the boatman who brought people into the land of the dead.

Tiny moon

Even asteroids can have moons. A spacecraft on its way to Jupiter passed the **asteroid** Ida. The asteroid is about 58 km (36 miles) long. Pictures sent back by the spacecraft showed that Ida has its own moon. A tiny chunk of space rock is orbiting it. The rock may have exploded from Ida when Ida was struck by a **meteorite**.

Charon is 1186 kilometres (737 miles) in **diameter**. That makes Charon half as big as Pluto. All other moons in the **solar system** are tiny compared to their planets. Astronomers call Pluto and Charon a double planet because of the closeness in size.

Charon orbits close to Pluto. It is only 19,600 kilometres (12,180 miles) away from the planet. It takes Charon a little more than six days to orbit Pluto once.

Astronomers know very little about Charon because it is so far away from the Earth. Astronomers believe hills of ice cover its surface. Charon may have a thin **atmosphere**. If there is an atmosphere on Charon, it most likely comes from Pluto.

NASA made this photograph from several photographs. It shows Jupiter and the four Galilean moons. The sizes and distances are not to scale.

Io

Europa

Ganymede

Callisto

Moons of Jupiter and Saturn

Four planets in our **solar system** are made mostly of gas. Like all planets, these giant planets **orbit** the Sun in a set order. Jupiter is the fifth planet from the Sun. It is followed by Saturn, Uranus and Neptune. Most moons in our solar system orbit around these gas giants.

Jupiter has 39 moons. Four of the moons are very large. These four moons are called Galilean moons. The famous **astronomer** Galileo discovered them in 1610. The other moons are tiny. In the 19th, 20th and 21st centuries, astronomers discovered them with new, more powerful **telescopes**.

Astronomers found Jupiter's seventeenth moon in July 2000. It was the first moon of Jupiter to be discovered in more than two decades. Since then, astronomers have discovered 22 new moons.

The surface of Callisto has more craters than any place in the solar system.

Callisto

Of the Galilean moons, Callisto is the furthest away from Jupiter. Callisto **orbits** Jupiter at a distance of about 1.9 million kilometres (1.2 million miles). This is about five times further than the Earth's Moon is from the Earth.

Callisto is the third largest moon in the **solar system**. It is almost as big as the planet Mercury. The moon is covered with dust-filled ice. **Meteorite craters** cover its whole surface.

Ganymede

Ganymede is the third furthest Galilean moon from Jupiter. It orbits Jupiter at a distance of about 1 million kilometres (620,000 miles). Ganymede is the largest moon in the solar system. It is 5262 kilometres (3270 miles) in **diameter**. This is larger than the planets Mercury and Pluto.

The USA sent the space probe *Voyager* to explore the solar system. A space probe is a spacecraft built to explore and gather information about space. In 1979, *Voyager* took pictures and recorded information about Ganymede. It sent this information back to scientists on the Earth.

Pictures from *Voyager* showed that Ganymede has many craters. The craters tell **astronomers** that the surface of Ganymede is very old. Younger moons have very few craters. Ganymede is roughly half rock and half ice. Its dark, icy surface is lined with cracks and grooves. Astronomers also think that Ganymede may have an ocean beneath its ice.

The *Galileo* spacecraft took this picture
of Europa. It has many cracks in its
smooth surface.

Europa

Europa is Jupiter's second closest Galilean moon. It
orbits at a distance of 670,900 kilometres (416,900
miles). Europa is the smallest of Jupiter's four Galilean
moons. It is 3138 kilometres (1950 miles) in **diameter**.
This is a little smaller than the Earth's Moon.

Europa is a bright moon. It reflects much of the sunlight that falls on it. A thin **atmosphere** surrounds Europa. The atmosphere has some oxygen, but not enough for people to live. People would have to bring their own oxygen to Europa to breathe.

Europa's surface is very smooth. It has very few **craters**, and these aren't very big. The largest are just a few kilometres wide.

Clear ice covers Europa's surface. **Astronomers** think Europa's ice may be floating on an ocean of water. Close-up pictures show many large grooves in the ice. There are also many cracks. Scientists think that the ice is broken into huge floating plates. If this is true, the markings are caused by huge ice plates drifting into each other. Europa's surface looks like a bunch of ice cubes that have frozen into one large block.

Any water under Europa's ice may be like the Earth's oceans. If so, this is the only other water ocean in the **solar system** that scientists have found so far. Some scientists think tiny forms of life may live in the water.

Io is the most volcanically active object in our solar system.

Io

Io is the closest Galilean moon to Jupiter. It is 3660 kilometres (2274 miles) in **diameter**. It takes only about 1.7 days to complete an **orbit** of Jupiter.

Voyager took pictures of Io and sent them back to the Earth. Io is a rocky ball with a red, orange and black surface. Some people compare the look of Io's surface to that of a huge cheese pizza.

Io is one of the few moons that has an **atmosphere**. Its atmosphere is mostly sulphur-dioxide gas. This gas is poisonous to people.

Many large, active volcanoes rise from Io's surface. These mountains form over cracks in the crust of a planet or moon. Ash, gas and melted rock called lava sometimes erupt, or blow out, of volcano openings. Volcanoes on Io often erupt ash, lava and sulphur. It is the sulphur that gives Io its colour. The volcanoes on Io also erupt huge clouds of sulphur-dioxide gas. Some of the erupted material falls back to the surface, and some of the volcanoes are surrounded by huge, smooth lakes of lava.

Volcano eruptions on Io blast some sulphur-dioxide gas into space. Some volcanoes explode columns of gas up to 450 kilometres (280 miles) high. As Io orbits Jupiter, some of the gas leaves a sulphur-dioxide trail. This creates a circle-shaped cloud of sulphur-dioxide gas surrounding Jupiter.

Titan

Beyond Jupiter, the giant ringed planet Saturn **orbits** the Sun. Saturn has 30 moons. Some **astronomers** think Saturn may have even more moons. Many of Saturn's known moons are only a few kilometres in **diameter**.

Titan is Saturn's largest moon. In fact, Titan is the second largest moon in the **solar system**.

Titan is one of the few moons in the solar system to have an **atmosphere**. Its atmosphere is thicker than the Earth's atmosphere. It is made up mostly of nitrogen gas. Titan's atmosphere does not have much oxygen. People would need to bring oxygen to breathe on Titan.

Astronomers cannot see the surface of Titan. Its atmosphere is too cloudy and orange. An orange haze from the gases in its atmosphere surrounds the moon.

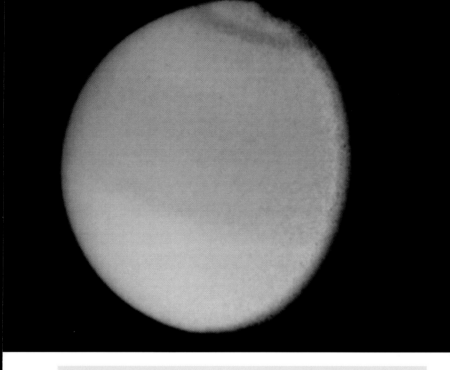

▲ Scientists believe that Titan may have
ethane and methane oceans on its surface.

The temperature at Titan's surface is about
−178°C (−288°F). This temperature is cold enough
to turn some of Titan's gas into liquid form. Some
astronomers think Titan may have a liquid-gas ocean.

Astronomers hope to learn more about the
surface of Titan. They plan to send the *Huygens*
space probe into Titan's atmosphere in 2004. The
probe will examine the gases in the atmosphere. It
will also take pictures of the surface of Titan.

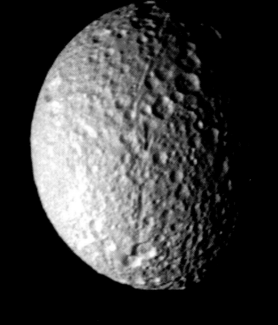

Mimas (top) was almost split in two by a large meteorite. The bottom photo shows the crater it made.

Mimas

Mimas is one of Saturn's smaller moons. It is about 418 kilometres (260 miles) in **diameter**. It **orbits** Saturn at a distance of 185,520 kilometres (115,282 miles).

The surface of Mimas is marked with many **craters**. One of the craters is 130 kilometres (81 miles) across. This is almost one-third of the diameter of Mimas. It is the largest surface feature on the moon. In places, the crater is 10 kilometres (6 miles) deep. This huge crater on Mimas was named Herschel Crater to honour the **astronomer** William Herschel. He discovered Mimas in 1789.

A great deal of heat was created when a huge **meteorite** hit Mimas and made the Herschel Crater. Heat from the explosion melted some of the rock. The melted rock splashed around the surface. Some of the rock splashed into the centre of the crater, then cooled and formed a mountain. The mountain in the crater is almost as high as Mount Everest. The central peak of the mountain is 6 kilometres (4 miles).

Saturn's rings

Moons are natural satellites of planets, but the gas planets also have rings. Rings are made up of millions of tiny rock and dust satellites. Most rings are small and difficult to see from the Earth.

Saturn has wide rings circling it. To early **astronomers**, the rings made the planet look as if it had ears. With better **telescopes**, astronomers saw the rings more clearly. They counted several wide rings.

The *Voyager* space probe flew past Saturn and took pictures of the rings. The pictures showed thousands of tiny rings which formed into bands of rings. From the Earth, the tiny rings together look like several big rings.

Saturn's rings are not solid bands. The rings are made of billions of rock particles. Each piece of rock is like a tiny moon **orbiting** the planet. The rock particles can be as small as pebbles or bigger than buses. The particles are close together and they all move in the same direction as they orbit Saturn. This makes the rings look solid, but they are not.

The nearest ring is about 67,000 kilometres (42,000) miles from the planet. The furthest rings are hundreds of thousands of kilometres from the planet.

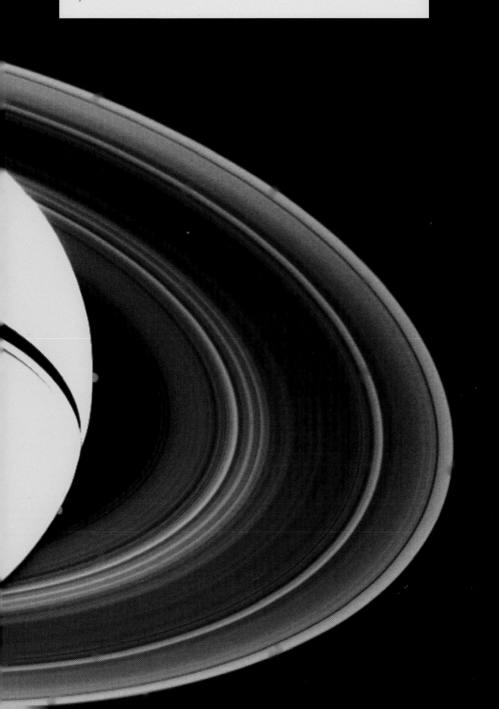

 Saturn's rings are made up of many pieces of rock and ice.

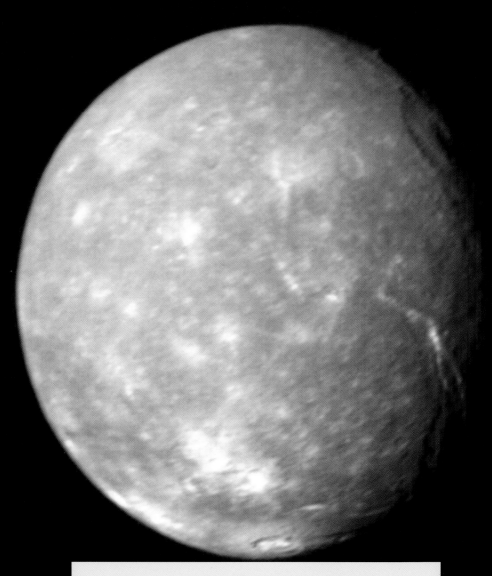

Titania is about 436,000 km (271,000 miles) away from Uranus.

The outer moons

Uranus has at least 20 moons. Most of Uranus's moons are very small. Many of the moons are less than 200 kilometres (120 miles) in **diameter**. Titania is Uranus's largest moon. It is about 1578 kilometres (980 miles) in diameter.

Like many other moons, Uranus's moons have many **craters**. The surfaces of most of them appear to be ice and rock. Most of the moons do not have volcanoes or oceans.

Miranda is one of Uranus's larger moons. It is about 470 kilometres (290 miles) in diameter. It is almost 130,000 kilometres (81,000 miles) away from Uranus. Large cliffs, canyons and grooves cover Miranda's surface. Scientists think that moonquakes made some surface features. A moonquake is a sudden shaking of the outer surface of a moon.

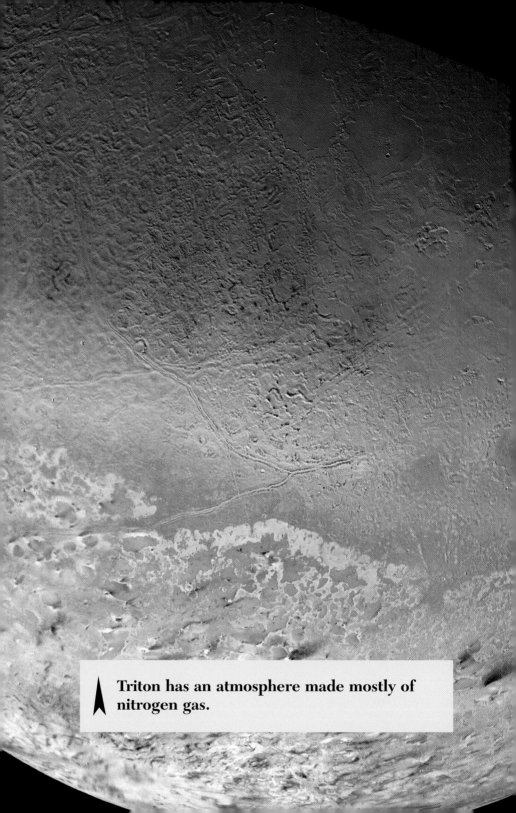

Triton has an atmosphere made mostly of nitrogen gas.

Neptune's moons

Neptune has eight known moons. It might have more moons that have not yet been discovered. Neptune is so far away that it is hard for **astronomers** to see.

Most of Neptune's moons are small. Many are less than 416 kilometres (259 miles) in **diameter**.

Neptune's largest moon is Triton. It is about 2700 kilometres (1700 miles) in diameter. Triton is about 355,000 kilometres (221,000 miles) away from Neptune.

The surface of Triton is covered with patches of frost-like frozen nitrogen gas. The surface has dark streaks where volcanoes and geysers have erupted dark material. Geysers are holes in the ground through which liquids and gases shoot out.

Triton has the lowest measured temperature of all the moons. Its surface is a frosty –235°C (–391°F). This is more than four times colder than Antarctica in winter. Antarctica is the coldest place on the Earth.

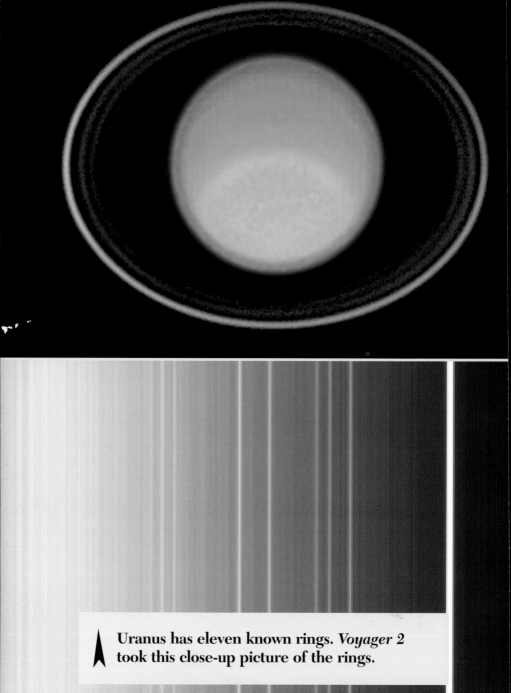

Uranus has eleven known rings. *Voyager 2* took this close-up picture of the rings.

Ring systems

Both Uranus and Neptune have ring systems. Uranus has eleven known rings and Neptune has four.

The rings of Uranus are very dark. They are made of rock pieces that are only a few metres wide.

The rings around Uranus give the planet a special appearance. Uranus is tilted on its side. The rings make the planet look like a bullseye. A person would have to travel near the planet by spacecraft to see the bullseye.

The four rings of Neptune look as if they are broken. Parts of the rings are bright, and others are very hard to see. Small pieces of rock and dust make up the rings. The pieces are not spread out evenly. Sections of rings with large clumps of pieces reflect light and look bright. Sections with only a few pieces do not reflect light and look like dark gaps.

More moons

Astronomers think our **solar system** might have even more moons. They are hoping to make new discoveries of moons **orbiting** planets.

Astronomers are sending new space probes into space. The space probes will explore new parts of the solar system. Astronomers will study the information from the probes to look for more moons.

Glossary

asteroid (AS-tuh-roid) giant space rock that orbits the Sun

astronomer scientist who studies objects in space

atmosphere layer of gases that surrounds an object in space

crater bowl-shaped hole left when a meteorite strikes an object in space

diameter distance from one side of a sphere or circle to the other, passing through the centre

gravity force that attracts one object to another; the gravitational force exerted by an object depends on its mass

meteorite (MEE-tee-or-rite) space rock that crashes into the surface of another object in space

orbit path an object takes as it travels around another object in space

solar system a star and all the objects that orbit around it

telescope instrument that makes faraway objects appear clearer and closer

Websites

BBC Science
http://www.bbc.co.uk/science/space/
British National Space Centre
http://www.bnsc.gov.uk/
European Space Agency
http://sci.esa.int/
**Star Child: A Learning Centre for
                    Young Astronomers**
http://starchild.gsfc.nasa.gov/

Books

Exploring the solar system: The Moon, Giles
    Sparrow (Heinemann Library, 2001)
The Universe: The Moon, Raman Prinja
    (Heinemann Library, 2002)

Useful address

London Planetarium
Marylebone Road
London
NW1 5LR

Index